AMERICAN
VALUES AND
DEVALUES

AMERICAN VALUES AND DEVALUES

JOHN O. HUNTER

AMERICAN VALUES AND DEVALUES

Author: Dr. John Hunter
Editor: Timothy DeWeen
Technical Assistance: Kim Flosson, Justin Perry, and Elaine DeWeen
Printed by Highland Park: Blake Aspardu, Facility Administrator

iUniverse books may be ordered through booksellers or by contacting:

iUniverse
1663 Liberty Drive
Bloomington, IN 47403
www.iuniverse.com
844-349-9409

ISBN: 978-1-6632-3552-7 (sc)
ISBN: 978-1-6632-3553-4 (e)

Print information available on the last page.

iUniverse rev. date: 03/18/2022

Contents

Preface

Until recently the USA was the world leader in Technological Development. It is now fading rapidly in this role due to administrative weakness and significant advances and threats by China and Russia. Many Americans are unaware of this rapid change, which only weakens us further.

This is the first of a series of articles designed to invoke understanding of the values and issues in technological development. All staff and residents are invited to submit their own perspectives as well as criticism and questions. Educational efforts by all of our institutions is vital to our national security and enhanced understanding. Highland Park acknowledges responsibility to observe and learn.

-JOH

I

The Power of Propaganda

The differences of pure art and propaganda art are exemplified many ways and times in popular writings. Two examples of powerful propaganda art are Karl Marx and Friedrich Engels' *The Communist Manifesto*, and Harriet Beecher Stowe's *Uncle Tom's Cabin*.

No question they both had enormous appeal and influence. Marx still has appeal in academic circles, but the systems he helped to spawn through communist ideology are now in the "ash heap of history." No communist revolution was brought off in the Marxist way, and his prophecy of the "withering away of the state" was always absurd.

Stowe's work is a somewhat different case. If there is such a thing as a great propaganda art, *Uncle Tom's Cabin* is it, but it does not tell the true story of slavery in the South. (A more reliable account is Nathalie Dessins', *Myths of the Slave Plantation*, 2003, or see WJ Cash, *The Mind of the South*, 1941.

Following her quick climb to celebrity status, Stowe was invited to visit the Scottish Highlands at the time of the "Clearances". While seeing more of Scotland than she did of Kentucky, she was unwittingly suborned by the Scottish aristocracy and became an accomplice in an evil on par with slavery. She wrote *Sunny Memories* as an account of her visit. Her utter naïveté and blindness to the terrible cruelties afflicted on the Highlanders at the hands of their own clan chiefs– certainly as bad or worse than southern slave masters– is graphically captured in John Prebble's *The Highland Clearances,* 1963.

As we sometimes say of people we like, "Mrs. Stowe had a good heart and her righteousness was worthy." But she had no talent for finding the truth. It is astonishing to realize that her single work is still considered by some college faculty as great literature, as I discovered in a conversation that rated *Uncle Tom's Cabi*n as a greater novel than Herman Melville's *Moby Dick*.

Ephemeral though it may be, propaganda is sometimes compelling indeed! In today's mass media and information systems it is a constant ferocious driver of public and self deception. The ideologies of cultural relativism and religious fanaticism often combine with propaganda to create further confusion and threaten chaos in the public realm.

Many journalists, politicians, and even educators do not understand or respect the normative values of personal integrity and dignity endowed by our Creator on all human beings. Mistaken conclusions about people's incapacity to discern truth are constantly made based on observations of intolerance and incivility. Historically, these have always been problems in democratic society, due in part to the freedom, missing in totalitarian regimes, given to propagandists and demagogues. But it is wrong to generalize from remarks of a bunch of rancorous or even malevolent individuals who have momentarily seized the spotlight.

When the individual citizen is left free to judge and to choose without fear of consequences, relying on his/her natural intelligence, the distinctions can be made between advocacy and analysis in the information presented. This may not always be the case, but mere propaganda need not win. It is an elitist mistake to underestimate the average person's intelligence.

We live in an ideological age that forges denial of the human soul's connection to truth and goodness. For many people it is still too much to grasp that there is an immutable moral law. Yet, for most people, even under the cynical weight of collective propaganda, a principled point of view is not beyond call.

Does not "good propaganda" have a positive effect? Possibly so, if it ripples the flow of action to good ends. But propaganda plays on the surface of things. It lacks the depth and authenticity of quest for truth— truth that through time will make a universal claim. So it was that despite their false doctrine of lies and propaganda, even harnessed to great political and literary power, Hitler's Third Reich, the Bolsheviks and the Soviet Union, Apartheid, and Saddam Hussein's Iraq, all fell in the short span of the 20th century.

And so we may believe in John Milton's *Areopagitica:*

"Though all the winds of doctrine were let loose to play upon the earth, so Truth be in the field, we do injuriously by licensing and prohibiting to doubt her strengths: let Truth and falsehood grapple; whoever knew Truth put to worse in a free and open encounter."

Notes on War on Women

Theodore Dalrymple, a brilliant psychiatrist (somewhat in the mold of Charles Krauthammer) tells the story of a young Muslim woman who wanted to go to work and live like a Western woman. In the eyes of her parents and brothers there could be no worse insult to the family, but eventually they gave way because they needed the money.

So this young woman who had been subdued all of her life went to work and in doing so found freedom. She loved her work which was a daily release from prison at home, the only time she was allowed out. The work was like air after suffocation. When I was president, I would have been glad to hire her and otherwise oppressed Muslim women to work for me. But that was not the attitude of her brothers who wanted westernized lives for themselves but not for their sisters. This may be explainable in a Muslim culture which does not value the autonomy and individuality of their women.

But what explains the attitude of our feminists who subscribe to the "war on women"? In our colleges and universities especially we see and hear them fearlessly fighting for speech codes and politically correct language (should we say "personhole" rather than "manhole cover"?) while their veiled sisters in the middle east continue to suffer oppression and physical abuse, including torture, and nary a word do we hear about it.

But of course we do know: it's all about ideology.

II

Flashpoints and Endpoints

"Despair is only for those who see the end beyond all doubt." (J.R.R. Tolkien)

Elsewhere I have argued the difference between physical evolution and spiritual evolution and the hope for a new ground being formed which authentically combines science and faith through the collaboration of human beings and super intelligent machines, coming soon in the invention of a brave new world. This will be the next flashpoint of evolution and the ultimate challenge of the next generation. If God is left out of the equation, the outcome will be *apocalyptic extremis*– with a bang or a whimper it won't matter– truly the End of Days.

My friends and I will not face it, but my grandchildren might. I wish that we could be of more support for them. I can only hope that genes of courage and integrity have passed on to them, and that they will bond with other like souls.

Let me enter a word of humility here: My current view is that nobody really knows anything. To accurately predict the future is an unreasonable quest, especially so for technological forecasting, but as the monks of Genesee Abbey know, our God is a God of love and sometimes, a God of surprises. Of all the institutional damages we have experienced in my lifetime, I grieve most the killing of "the liberal arts tradition." in our colleges and universities. I would not recommend for any potential student what is left of this once supremely valuable program. I say this with gratitude for my own liberal arts matriculation many years ago in the hands of admirable professors.

One introduced me to literary criticism, another to the Socratic method – both aimed at search for the truth – and a third to history of civilization (which he sometimes taught in Latin.) Others sressed the connection of good writing and logic. There was no fierce political indoctrination such as we have today! I liked and trusted all of my teachers.

These "scholars and gentlemen/ladies" could move a circle of students to ardent discussion of factual knowledge, and very importantly, issues and value differences, without rancor or hyperbole– or at least, if these distractions came up, would try to restore the circle's integrity. By no means did they seek conformity of opinion. While I was not an all star student in those days, almost inadvertently I discovered something magnificent that set me on a course eventually to become my professional life. It is a process of rational inquiry and dialectical arrival at conclusions.

Keep three skills in balance: Inquiry, Acknowledgment, Advocacy. There is truth to be found but none of us will ever have sole possession of it. You never know what you don't know.

We see the world from our own perspectives. Each of us has our own story. Learning someone else's story or side of the issue may let us see something we didn't see before. In this learning conversation we ask questions about the information– examine the empirical data– trace our interpretations of it.

The process goal is always the same: **what is the truth**? Not what is most popular– or what is easiest to accept– or what or who will win an election?

Socrates stressed humility in the face of truth, but there is also room for enthusiasm! In fact, without it you can't get very far. The method does not rob you of your advocacy but it will test your assumptions and interpretations, strengthening or refining or amending them, helping you to clarify your position. The conversation ends with acknowledgment that there may still be something missing, something more to learn. At the same time if we are responsible for making a decision, we do not shrink from the responsibility. Rather we trust in our informed judgment.

Tough, honest criticism is essential, but throughout the process there is respect for the other guy or gal. It's demonstrated by acknowledging each other's position. To acknowledge of course is not the same thing as to agree. We may achieve a synthesis, or it may be that we simply agree to disagree, at least for the present. Without mutual understanding of the process it will simply stop. Embarrassed, friendly adversaries withdraw to the protection of banality; others may resort to violence.

In my youthful naïveté, it did not occur to me that such a beautiful approach could be undermined by our culture or threatened by another culture of death. Now there is something happening in our culture as it interacts with fantastic ideology which is threatening the process of rational inquiry and coarsening the dialogue.

Within our presumed democratic society, the decline of rational method and the resulting instability is traceable to both political excess and cultural fascination with image making and entertainment in which image is more important than truth.

We are bombarded mercilessly by images of all kinds, but the significant force is the image bending, the manipulation, distortion, even lies by professional media handlers and politicians who are very skilled and clever. They can turn the world upside down, building a mountain of irrationality– an Orwellian world– in which we are also witnessing a clash of civilizations.

Evils of the 20th century continued and exploded in the 21st with a significant twist: Much of the evil done now is freely chosen and not even characterized as such. I do not contend that government is the monster, but neither is government blameless for what now afflicts every country and has brought pain and suffering to its high peak.

It began with ideologies propounded by intellectuals, especially the idea that man/woman should be freed from the shackles of social convention and self-control. Anything goes. Our governments in the West responded by enacting laws that promoted unrestrained behavior and created welfare systems that protect people from their personal decisions.

There was a time, I can remember it, when chivalry would not sanction torture of women and children; transgressors were branded as cowards; the despots who fostered it would eminently deny their actions. Now, torture of the worst kind against innocents is standard practice with some governments and freely admitted, even boasted about.

Why do we have this rising tide of cruelty and joyous malignity that staggers but does not appease human imagination for inhumanity? Is it the poverty? No that is the biggest canard! In a time of much less prosperity not so long ago, such conduct was much less widespread; the evil was contained to evil men.

Metaphorically speaking, it may be seen as a legacy of Original Sin. Contemporaneously, it is better explained as far ranging moral cowardice, justified because we know now that everyone is entitled to their own opinion and their own way of life. In the decline of the West there is no scale of human values as there once was. The winning argument on the international scene is moral equivalence.

Though I now observe from the outside, the evidence suggests that some of today's professors, not all but too many, are more interested in particular ideologies than they are in objective scholarship and balanced search for the truth and justice. What happened?

How did the current orientation to ideology become so strong that many of these "educators" do not even know they are caught in an ideological trap?) I suspect that Schools of Education and "student development" staff members have a lot to do with it. I saw it first, taken by surprise, in England in the mid-1980s when scandalous means to control who would be allowed to speak in public forums and lectures emerged. Essentially unchallenged, this fascism metastasized and is now rampant in American as well as British universities.

I did not experience it in Alfred in the 80s, and there may still be other small colleges which hold on to the traditional values of academe, but I fear that many of our colleges and universities have lost their way. Too many college administrations are feckless in dealing with assaults on campus freedom and institutional integrity.

I do not know how true this is of our grade schools. I have two daughters who teach in elementary school and are committed to their students and do not share my trepidation. I was amazed when a small group of the students from a poor environment eagerly accepted a gift of classic books. I am glad for these tokens, so I want to be cautious here, but we need to acknowledge some serious problems that interfere drastically with student growth and development today, including a wretched drug culture our kids face that exceeds anything we knew in my youth.

Heroin is cheaper than many painkillers and is easily accessible even in small NY towns like Hornell and Canaseraga, a phenomenon unknown in the Griffin Manor housing project where I grew up.

Big Pharma rules: America is now a fully loaded drug addiction society beginning with drugs prescribed every day at pharmacies, used/abused at hospitals, and introduced to children at an early age (Ritalin). Parents and counselors are astonished to realize how quickly the addiction can happen. A teenager may be neck-deep in drug addiction and completely unable to break away on his/her own.

Equally troublesome (and scary) is emphasis on social media: Have you ever watched a bunch of teen-agers sitting on a couch but not bothering to converse with each other, too absorbed in listening to a cell-phone connection ? – portent of a superficial plasticised existence?

III

Love of Truth

We know that we live in a material world which compels us to stay with rational interpretations and logical discovery– the scientific method. Angels around us, faeries living with us, visions of an alternative existence, parallel universes– these notions are easily dispelled even though we frequently find them on our entertainment channels. They continue to have credence. Actually they have been in our minds for a long time, longer than the age of science.

So how do we know the truth of anything? Some philosophers tell us that the truth is totally subjective: We do not live in the world, we live in a picture or vision of it that we have formed. Others say that truth is external and objective. On the extreme end is the "true believer" who not only knows that he has the whole truth but is responsible to see that others accept it also.

But the lover of truth I believe is somewhere in between: He or she comes to recognize that the truth of anything is measured slowly, yet the desire for it is universal.

The lover of truth does not confuse sincerity or passion with truth. He or she is aware that it is easy to be deceived, especially by ourselves. The search is not easy. Lies and bad faith may not always appear as such; they may wear the mask of truth.

Truth is aive; it grows and deepens as a person develops. What was true at 20 may have new meaning at 50. Truth is not just an accumulation of "facts" though these may be essential in the discovery process. I find companions for truth in poets such as WB Yeats and Robert Burns; in saints such as Patrick and John Paul; and in forgotten American leaders such as Crazy Horse and Chief Joseph. They break through conventional worldviews.

When I was growing up my teachers sought to put me on the right track by demythologizing or "debunking" everything. I learned that anything mythical was false, unreal, unhistorical or unscientific. A "myth" corresponded to a lie. I realize now what a disservice it was to me personally when I bought into this crimped way of looking at the world. To impart culture as though history is what happened and myth is fiction distorts our understanding of who we are and where we come from.

I see how powerful the myth is and how essentially true and fundamental to a coherent, sane explanation of reality it may be. In America we share many myths which shape our sense of national consciousness and even our destiny.

One of the most prevalent is the "American Dream."

Usually it means the chance for a better life in America, upward mobility, the opportunity to succeed through hard work, "pulling us up by our own bootstraps," the idea of reinventing oneself, living in a land of law and order. In the past two decades, this myth has been downplayed.

Some faculty go out of their normal curriculum to dispel the myth of the American Dream. They want a different ideological orientation that often seems to translate to "Hate America" stuff.

I believe this attitude is a cancer not only on the spirit of America but on the institutions which hold her up and focus on the important work of trying to solve long term problems, including the racial divide. America is not a racist nation: We could not have elected a black president if that were true, but it would be foolish to say that we do not have serious racial issues. Rightly understood and fostered, the American Dream could be used as an effective cultural tool in the struggle for ~~e Pluribus Unum.~~ For a long time it has been but now seems to be threatened by other emerging ideological myths, such as "Black Lives Matter."

Mistaken ideology by some college presidents and their student life administrators, that students should be worried about language that might violate campus rules or "hurt the feelings" of other students is a harbinger for violent censorship and a platform for continuing mob attacks. If today's authorities continue to foster the notion that silencing opponents is what good people do, the time is coming when dissenters on college campus will be beaten and even murdered. The ideologies of moral authoritarianism and identity politics will replace our once dearly embraced ideals of liberty and justice, and even well-intentioned radicals will not understand the wreckage they have wrought, or know what has happened to their institutions.

IV

Mythology and Victimology

The Orestian Myth

We know from recent advances in our study of different cultures, and thanks to leading thinkers such as Carl Jung that a myth persists – that is, it is a myth– precisely because it is true. The same myths are found in culture after culture throughout the ages.

I don't mean to say that they are literally true– there is a good deal of symbolism involved with myths– but they are true in what they tell us about human nature and the human condition. We may find a truth about ourselves in a myth;sometimes, we must dig to find that truth, but the digging is worthwhile.

Of course, it's important to be able to recognize a myth. There are big differences between the myth and a fairytale. For example, Santa Claus, who has been around only for a couple hundred years, is just a fairytale. Likable though he may be, he will never make it to the status of myth.

In his book, The Road Less Traveled, M. Scott Peck uses the myth of Orestes to discuss healthy personality. This is another of the myths associated with the Trojan Wars in ancient Greece.

As Peck explains, Orestes was a young man caught in a great moral dilemma when he discovered that his mother had murdered his father. The greatest obligation that a young Greek boy had was to avenge the murder of his father. On the other hand, the worst imaginable thing that he could do was to kill his mother. Following up on his obligation to avenge his father Orestes did kill his mother. Of course he had to pay a terrible price.

Pursued relentlessly by the Furies who would not let him escape from bad dreams and hallucinations, he was in continual torment until finally he prayed to the gods that they have mercy and release him. The gods held a trial for Orestes, and the Sun God, Apollo, represented him.

Apollo presented a defense that we hear used a lot today. Apollo said that what Orestes had done was not really his fault. Orestes, he said, had been placed in a terrible situation not of his choosing; he was a victim of circumstance and should not be held responsible.

Then something splendid and sensational happened: Orestes stood up and rejected Apollo's defense. No, he said, the truth is that I am responsible and I must bear the consequences.

The gods were amazed. This was the first time a mere mortal had accepted responsibility for his own actions, and the gods, who are used to being blamed for everything, decided to free him.

But there is even more. Orestes was not just restored. The Furies who had been persecuting him were replaced by three angels who were bearers of "grace and light." From out of the torment and sickness unto death, Orestes was brought to extraordinary health and wisdom.

V

Vandals, Desperadoes, and Heroes

Did you ever think you would see what is now happening on our college campuses?– masked radicals punching women in the stomach? spitting and throwing feces? campus police asked to stand down while radicals vandalize buildings, set fire to classrooms, wreck automobiles, break windows?

Granted, many of the violaters are professional agitators, rather than students, all the more reason to enforce the law on campus. Time for BMOCS and WMOCS to intervene, college heroes, get up and get to it in a brave and orderly way. The vandals and desperadoes do not own the college!

Worst of all is that some college administrators simply stand aside ; some will even defend the chaos.

Who are these guys? not just the agitators but the administrators, who seem to be so weak and indecisive – not all, but enough of them to ask, "what do you think you're doing?" Are they just flying on the wings of ideology?

Hey, colleagues of mine, those who remember how optimistic we were about academic life 40 to 50 years ago: You may agree that the erosion of academic freedom and free speech on our college campuses today, obviously spreading, is the major threat to higher education, and perhaps to America as a whole.

In the 1960s, when young guys like me first entered into the arena, we still had the historical examples of what I consider to be the royalty of higher education, Harvard's Charles W. Elliott, Chicago's Robert M. Hutchins, Samuel P. Capen, University of Buffalo, and other presidents and professors who spoke with a strong sense of values, spiritual as well as intellectual. Then the inspiration of Jacques Barzun, the premier model of a scholar and gentleman! (His book, *Teacher in America, put me on solid ground in my first year of teaching, I am forever grateful.)* Most of my professors seemed to be of that mold. Students of my generation who became my colleagues saw a field of promise that streched out for our years ahead.

What happened? Why were these rocks pushed aside? When I became president, I began to see the decline of liberal arts tradition and objective scholarship. There was a steady rise of the "isms"– – Marxism(even in English classrooms), Feminism, Freudianism, Deconstructionism – – cascading and running over the historic values of the pursuit of knowledge – – beauty, truth, the good. It began to seem that these purposes of liberal learning were shoved into a category of hopeless naïveté. They were also being jammed by political correctness and cultural relativism, now today claiming supremacy.

Where are the college presidents who should be defending academic values and upholding the law?. Whoever and wherever they are, I don't hear much about them.. Too often, what is coming across to the public is weakness, lewdness, denigration of our Constitution, and ridicule of historical achievements– a stream of invective and hyperbole that so far seems to go on without challenge except for a few courageous organizations, such *as National Association of Scholars(NAS), American Council of Trustees and Alumni (ACTA),*

FIRE, Young Americans for Freedom(YAF), Academic Leadership Council. Thank God for them and their allies.

Here I want to single out a few of the top organizations:Do we need leaders who will continue to distinguish First Amendment ideas from new options promoted for thought control? Do we need objective monitoring of blatant attempts to coerce students' political persuasion and affiliation? This is the mission and role of the NAS, as well as ACTA and YAF, aimed at focusing on the accountability of some of the major universities in our land.

The young people and seniors in these organizations are the true warriors and patriots, defending not only higher education but America as a whole in a time of national crisis.

What's behind all of the chaos? I believe it stems mainly from the Marxist orientation of radical left-wing professors who are striving to capture a "progressive" high ground for revolution that seeks to purge historic liberal balance, an "alienation of the intellectuals" that the eminent historian, Crane Brinton, posited as the first stage of revolution in his classic work, *Anatomy of Revolution.*

Why are there so few cool-headed folks on the academic front lines now? What happened to the old balanced engagement of "I disagree with you, but I will contend for your right to be wrong - - let's go get a beer and try to work it out."

Let's be clear and honest about it:There is a serious problem of teacher incompetency in secondary and post-secondary education, and an even greater problem of too many staff assistants who do not contribute to an educational mission. The resources spent there would be better used for the purpose of teaching kids at least to write a complete sentence.

The fault lies with Boards and administrations that were not alert to an Orwellian invasion, wrought primarily by Dewey- soaked schools of education and state agencies, but aided and abetted by our own lack of courage to stand up to assaults on institutional integrity and academic standards.

Yet somehow I do not feel despair: We are facing a crisis, but I remain confident that there is a residual cadre of committed professionals in education who could right the ship if they would step up to answer the call for meaningful reform.

As for the progressives, not all radical thinkers are deluded or to blame for the extremism of their colleagues. But it seems to me that too much of the language and action now unfolding is putting us on a slippery slope. Too many of our students and some of their professors are opting for violence, and so I worry more than I did before.

In my view, a lot of the dissonance is due to the media complex that loves to stir things up for ratings. What happened to the old professional journalism that tried to be impartial and thus helped us in a search for the truth? Has it been sunk by ideological warfare? Can we recover from the polarization and enjoy once again the honor and thrill of an objective teaching-learning process? I am confident that what we have seen in recent years is not a long-term trend. I believe that we can and shall recover from the progressive insurrection.

In my 50 years of mixing with college faculties, a few were knotheads, and may have claimed progressive identity, but the majority I knew were astute professors and teachers, truly committed to their students and their institution, competent in their disciplines, and good citizens. It's not possible that we have lost them all, but it's obvious that we need new leadership.

Some of that leadership will come in reminders of our personal autonomy and moral identity from new professors on the scene, such as Jordan Peterson of Toronto University. He sets a new tone, and others will follow.

VI

Leadership and Accountability

When I was College President, I was always talking about the "OD approach." I don't know how much of it survived me. In retrospect, I wonder how many of my listeners asked themselves, what's he talking about? OD? overdose? overdrive? I recall a humorous report back following presentation of the Blake and Mouton managerial grid, asking that we all strive to be 9/9 administrators. Does he mean that we should all work 9 to 9?

I think I did get through eventually, but there was nothing fancy about it. It's a matter of demanding competency and integrity, both personal and professional, and a willingness to be accountable.

From what I observe today, college presidents are managers, not leaders. They strive to survive and are too subservient to the political expectations of their faculty.

As a leader, the president, and other leading administrators, must lay down some basic principles and concepts that establish a values framework for the organization. I constantly pushed these:

- A student is not an interruption of our work: he/she is the purpose of it.

- Don't complicate the teaching process, back it up! Simplify and streamline procedures as much as possible.

- Expect integrity in all relationships; when reporting a mistake tell the whole truth of it; above all, don't tolerate dishonesty or lies.

- Don't rely on memos to solve problems, and don't try to fix the blame, fix the problem.

- Responsibilities should not be energized by exhortation or propaganda, but by clearly laid out duties and expectations.

- The key to good staff performance is training; a well-trained staff member will claim the job as his/her own.

- Be a strong advocate for a principled organization with a clear mission and honest people willing to accept accountability in carrying it out.

Saving America

The salvation of the America we know is not with our colleges and universities. It is in the loyalty and good will of ordinary Americans who still believe in America, work hard, love their families, and continue to practice their faith as Christians, Jews, Muslims, even those who do not confess their religious faith– it's getting harder, but these good people have not yet given up:

They need a boost of greater respect for Truth from those who have vowed to lead!

We do not need lessons from an elite band of progressive philosophers or fake news artists or movie stars, dull as ditchwater. We have in our history, groups that exemplify crossing over heroically from tragedy to revival and exoneration and new life purpose and national pride. Some of this history lies with Native American tribes, unfortunately almost completely unknown to the public.

Crazy Horse and Chief Joseph were patriots as honed to the ideas of freedom, liberty and justice as any of the founders of the new nation. Their tragedy stems from the white invaders' belief that they and their way of life had to be crushed in order that the new nation might spread and flourish. Thus ensued America's genocidal movement that none of the Founding Fathers would have approved.

On the walls of the library of Oglala Lakota College in Kyle, South Dakota there is an impressive array of photographs of Oglala young men who served their country in the military forces.

This is a remarkable story. These young Indian Braves began to call America their country, honor the flag, and join the U.S. military less than a generation after Wounded Knee and the end of the massacres. Stories of their courage in combat despite prejudice against them are intriguing and inspiring.

In the last century Native Americans consistently sent more men per capita into the U. S. Armed Forces than any other racial or ethnic group.

One Indian war story that stirred my heart is about Private Clarence Spotted Wood from North Dakota. He was born in 1914, entered the Army in 1942, went overseas in August 1944, and was killed December 21, 1944 in Luxembourg. On January 28, 1945 a memorial service was held in his honor. He had instructed his tribe: "If I should be killed and you have a memorial service, I want soldiers to go ahead with the American flag, I want cowboys to follow, all on horseback, I want one of the cowboys to lead the wildest of our horses with saddle and bridle on, I will be riding that horse." The service was carried out according to his instructions.

My conclusion is that the warrior spirit strong in the blood and culture of the Plains Indians could not die but was transferred to the service of the people who had taken their lands. This may not seem rational or just to those who want logical explanations, but we serve a God of surprises who allows Truth to wind its own path whatever our intentions.

It's a great irony that Native Americans, their lands having been stolen by the white man, became cowboys. The grand myth of the American cowboys and Indians has been played out all over the world. It's the story of the American frontier where the dialectics of America's development were fashioned.

Scots and American Indians

The history of the Scottish Highlanders is marked by their devotion to the land and expression of fighting spirit. I submit that the American Indian (or as some prefer, Native American) was cast from the same mold as the Scottish Highlander.

The tribal social structure with chieftain authority was similar to the Scottish clans. There was savagery but no worse than the European variety. In both tribal and clan culture there was a strong sense of honor, loyalty, family responsibility, and focus on justice.

The Indian had no concept of private property and could not understand how the land could be bought and sold. But again, is this not similar to the Scot cotters' idea that whatever else happened, the land would always be there for them?

As the American West opened up, there was a serious ground of difference between the white man and the red man about land ownership and responsibility that triggered enormous tragedy. In other respects I believe these men could have been brothers and could have found ways to avoid the genocide and the great devastation of nature that marked the 19th century.

Could it all have been done differently in ways that would have synthesized and harmonized the best common values and preserved our natural wealth? Yes, we can see that now in the aftermath, and perhaps there is some salvation through restoration efforts of sterling organizations such as *Earthjustice, Natural Resources Defense Council, National Wildlife Federation, Audubon, Nature Conservancy, and Sierra Club.*

VII

A Valorous Citizenship

I was pondering the following potential disasters as to whether or not we could survive them as United States of America:

nuclear war

massive grid failure

devastating monetary collapse

virtual reality trapping our souls while the natural environment continues to decline

the coming of thinking, self replicating machines

American Civil War II

My personal conclusion is that the country is still strong enough to manage these crises and survive in some form, though perhaps not to our liking, except for the last which would mean the end of our nation.

For a civil war to break out enough people must perceive the situation as unbearable and be willing to use violence. The police must be unwilling or unable to keep the sides apart. Do we have these conditions? Is there evidence of grave danger of their development?

Why do I believe that Americans united could survive any of the potential disasters we are facing in 2018?

Because we are an **exceptional nation** despite the hard left's ongoing efforts to deny our culture and constitutional government. **We are a valorous people who have demonstrated time and again the courage and resiliency to overcome crisis and continue to forge a unique national identity that has made this country the envy of many others.**

I make this claim despite the historic egregious errors of our American government.

We see it in the splendid formulation and development of U.S. Constitutional Democracy. Radical Leftists desire to erase this identity and substitute it with they know not what!– merely shows the vapid vision which seeks to bring America to its knees.

We see it in the beginnings of "environmentalism", our national parks, and transportation systems

We can see it in the WWII response of "the Greatest Generation"– the emergence of Rosie the Riviter and the Boys of Pointe Du Hoc– seminal events in our 20th century history.

We can see it in the bravery of police and firefighters who ran toward rather than away from the explosians of 9/11 and in the call of my young friend in Pennsylvania, Todd Beamer, "Let's Roll."

And we see it again in the intrepid spirit of those Southern folks (neighbors all) dealing with the devastation of Hurricanes Harvey and Irma –and further shown in the marvelous support given from citizens all across the nation.

Yes, we have a valorous citizenship! But it is currently deeply divided and not happy with its government.

We have allowed ourselves to be split by poisonous politics and Orwellian doctrine that move us closer to the brother against brother phenomenon of our 1860's Civil War.

WHAT, ME WORRY?

I want to agree with those who say "nothing like that could happen in today's America."

But wait! I worry to think this is just head in the sand philosophy that does not understand how catastrophes are triggered by events that can produce unimagined turmoil. If we have not thought through the possibilities, it is no good later *to "cry havoc."*

It is not my intention here to be a scaremonger, but I refuse to cast aside my duty as a free citizen in a God gifted country to think through our issues and challenges and strive for clarity, even if it seems impossible to arrive there. So I want to take on here, as an example, the realistic threat of massive grid failure caused by "electromagnetic pulses" (EMP)* without any claim to science/techology expertise. I am just a reporter, hoping to find clarity.

VIII

EMP: A Triggering Catastrophe

A letter from Prof. Richard Andres of National Defense University explains that **electromagnetic pulse, EMP**, can take two forms: the first comes from extreme solar activity, the second from an enemy detonated nuclear weapon above the atmosphere in the purposive attempt to create an EMP. The origins are different, but either could be catastrophic for the U.S.:

"Research also determined that our systems are unable to respond effectively to an event that knocks out power to a large region or the nation as a whole... Because virtually all financial transactions and communications are now conducted electronically, without electricity regions would lose the ability to buy, sell, and communicate instantly. ...Most individuals would lose access to food and medicine after around three days. Law enforcement would cease to exist in most localities within a week... Over a year the effects of a nationwide blackout would approach the level of a limited nuclear war."

Prof. Andres concludes that because the Grid is owned and regulated by so many different companies and group, it is the individual states rather than the federal government, that are responsible for protecting against EMP.

It is not easy to assess the probability of EMP occurring in the future, and no one likes to imagine the effects. So it is probably easy, with so many other detectable problems, to ignore this disaster possibility. It is also not hard to recognize that this could be an enormous mistake.

What are the implications for action? First and foremost, as the National Defense University analysis contends, it is up to state and local governments to enact regulations to protect against EMP threats to the Grid. Companies should be required by law to protect themselves. Local communities should have at least some amount of local renewable power generation capabilities that they can fall back on to keep emergency services running during the outage.

Some may say that all of this bureaucratic regulation, which is often unreliable in the first place, will be expensive– probably true. Yet in the face of a real EMP disaster, preparation costs would be negligible in comparison.

If it should occur, I believe the American spirit would kick in again, but I also believe it is simply foolish to depend on this solitary escape.

I believe it is natural for us to pray against it, but if it should occur, the impact would be so harrowing and the tendency to cast blame in all directions so overwhelming, that the unexpected force of it could trigger Civil War.

Such a national catastrophe would be abetted by radical left leaders who would welcome it as the launching of their Socialist agenda for a new America unshackled from the traditional values and institutions they hate and seek to destroy.

IX

Bureaucratic Ineptitude and Lies

"Political language… is designed to make lies sound truthful and murder respectable, and to give an appearance of solidity to pure wind." (George Orwell)

Freedom is under assault in the USA today in unprecedented ways. Corruption in various forms is now rampant, and almost everybody knows it. For those apologists who contend that this has always been true, it may be easy to make this claim in isolated cases but not to same degree, particularly in those institutions relied upon for check and balance, such as our universities, mainstream press, our financial institutions, the Justice Department, State Department, and the White House itself.

Pin blame on bureaucratic incompetence: God knows the IRS, Veterans Affairs, Land Management, EPA, etc. have much to answer for; but ultimately accountability lies with those who wield top level federal authority and power, including the Attorney General, Senate and House Leaders, and the President of the United States.

I have studied and taught and wrote about our history and government and been involved in institutional governance for many years, and have never felt this way before, even during the sad times of the Vietnam War.

Shadow Government

There is a growing concern among many citizens, myself included, about the massive growth of government and its evolution to a shadow government, not elected by the people, what some call "the deep state."– undetectable, hard to describe, but worrisome that it is more than just the problem of bureaucratic incompetence. Our federal government has grown far from what the Founding Fathers intended in the Constitution. In 1954, Sen. William Jenner warned about it:

"Today the path to total dictatorship in the US can be laid by strictly legal means, unseen and unheard by Congress, the President, or the people. Outwardly we have a constitutional government. We have operating within our government and political sphere, a well-organized political action group in this country, determined to destroy our Constitution and establish a one-party state. The important point to remember about this group is not its ideology but its organization. It operates secretly, silently, continuously to transform our government. This group is answerable neither to the president, the Congress, nor the courts. It is practically irremovable."

I am still evaluating the worth of this speech. If it were a definitive appraisal, in my view we would already have reached the border line of the end of days. I do not subscribe to conspiracy theories, but neither do I suggest that we should simply dump Sen. Jenner's argument as irrelevant.

Whatever the facts of it are, it will be a challenge to root it out and restore confidence that we still have government *for the people, by the people, of the people,* and yes, your vote really does count!

The situation is not hopeless!

We should not underestimate the talents and courage and insights of those young people who yearn for a principled government of integrity and honesty. Some may have been led into hypocrisy and deceit, but they are not all "snowflakes." Like most of us, I believe they detest the lies coming out of the mouths of power-hungry politicians. They are caught in a cruel dillemma – – the same old greed, violence and hatred masked by pseudonyms class struggle, racial struggle.

I have worked with the 16-25 age group my whole life and know their essential character: they want friends and are quick to bond w/each other in honesty and fairness; they are united by respect for freedom and equality – intrinsic American values. Sadly, they are being let down by some of their professors who have opted for ideology of class conflict and identity politics– rather than education– threatening to tear us apart as enemies.

Once again, as Orwell warned us, the lie has come upon us.

The liar does not always go straight for the throat ; he/she may ask only for allegiance to the lie, for complicity in the lie, respect for some alleged greater purpose that excuses the lie.

The simple redeeming act of a courageous man or woman is not to take part in the lies. The young man or woman trying to find truth even while recognizing that the search for truth is sometimes a thicket of difficulty, my faith tells me will have God on his/her side.

I think they and all of us need to be reminded of the words of our greatest president, Abraham Lincoln:

"We are not enemies but friends. We must not be enemies. Though passion may have strained it must not break our bonds of affection. The mystic chords of memory stretching from every battlefield and patriot grave to every living human heart and hearthstone all over this broad land, will yet swell the chorus of the union, when again touched, as surely they will be, by the better angels of our nature."

X

The Girls of Tehran

"Thank heaven for little girls
they grow up in the most delightful way."

Delara Derabi was 22 years old in Iranian prison, so now she would
have been in her mid 30s, with children of her own, a talented leader
in her Muslim community.

I keep pondering why her life was so mercilessly and cruelly and
senselessly ended when she had so much to give to her people. Why
did the women of her community not come to her aid?

I am intrigued by the basic question of why these girls of Tehran
took on the role of moral leadership? When their male brothers and
fathers retreated, they held their ground, never free of humiliation
or the threat of being flogged and thrown into prison for "their own
education and protection." In the streets it is best that they not be
seen nor heard, keeping eyes focused on the ground, not daring to
look at passersby. Asar Nafisi, author of Reading Lolita in Tehran
(2003) explains that the streets are patrolled by militia called the
Blood of God to make sure that women wear their veils properly,
do not wear makeup, and do not walk in public with men who are
not their fathers, brothers or husbands. At any moment they may be

hurled into a patrol car, taken to jail, flogged, forced to wash toilets and humiliated in other perverse ways. The humiliation of women stems from new sharia law that lowered the age of marriage from 18 to 9, reinstated stoning as punishment for adultery and prostitution, as well as other offenses not clearly defined.

Delara Derabi was sentenced to prison when she was 17, accused of murdering an elderly relative. She was hanged even though she had been given a temporary stay of execution by the Chief Justice. A British journalist reported, "she phoned her mother on the day of her hanging to beg for help and the phone was snatched by a prison official who said, we will easily execute your daughter and there's nothing you can do about it"...." Mother I can see from my window the scaffold where they are going to hang me."

Why do some Muslim women seek to justify honor killings, and forced marriages?

Well, we still have the brave girls of Tehran! Against the massive forces of paranoia, cruelty, and legally validated persecution and violence against women, they are still telling us that this is not a time for hopelessness and despair.

More penetrating, what nameless, inscrutable, unearthly thing is it that causes a man or woman or an entire community to savage and destroy their own children? What explains our own indifference to the suffering of little girls?

Is it really 'nameless'? Can it be explained in simple religious argument as the 'problem of evil"? Is it enough to say that Satan fell out of heaven to ravage God's creation?

I claim no authority on these matters, but I think we must go back millennial times and forces ago in God's creation of the world, from the time he said "Let There Be Light," through all the planetary invention and stardust, space potentiality soaring across an endless pre-biological vista, rainbow clusters of stars turned into nebulas, extraordinary shapes that defy description, indescribable colors, through further reaches of space emanating with the hum of celestial music, and black holes where nothing ever escapes, to the heavens where God releases his dialectical purpose, and a stage is set for His image projection, maybe not the only one, for the kind of life we know.

In blackness evil was born, blackness, all blackness, the primordial existence of natural/material things spurred on to its mysterious development by the immutable principle of "grow or die." God allowed evil to come into the world.

God works through an evolutionary process involving time. Evangelicals seem to insist that the substance of the Trinity could not have evolved; it had to be there from the beginning. Does it not seem to fit the Logos better that God was impersonal and naturally indifferent in the first stage of the universe He was creating?

The natural order came first, and then came what is referred to in the Nicene Creed as the "Holy Spirit, the Lord, the giver of life." This Spirit, as Jesus himself called it, is distinguished from the all powerful Creator and bears no responsibility for the natural order of things. The world was a given.

"In the beginning was the word...
And the word was made flesh...
And dwelt among us...
We have seen his glory
who came from the Father
full of grace and truth." (Gospel of John)

We cannot know how or when exactly: the human creature became self aware— knowing that he knew– thus the emergence of the human soul! For God the Creator it may have been an act similar to the emergence of the first flower: For millions of years vegetation rioted on the earth without flowers; then one morning a flower appeared and soon thereafter this miracle covered the planet in a blaze of glory. It would also be so with humans.

This Deity, sprung from the First, and merciful and caring whereas the First, in a vascular recess of power and majesty was not, became a part of human consciousness imparting an awareness of the Divine Presence and making us forever capable of faith and hope and love.

In framing this miracle, I realize that I am a heretic in the eyes of many followers of Christ Jesus. But I believe I am faithful to truth, as God leads me, in this attempt to reconcile rational understanding and acceptance of the divine mystery...even in the context of trying to find an answer to the evil done to the girls of Tehran and countless others.

I accept the possibility of my error but to finish, I cannot accept any idea of forgiveness or an apologetic for those bastards who raped and brutalized little girls: They need to rot in hell!

My books on Chasing Crazy Horse are full of episodes of betrayal of Native Americans and the land they revered. There are many environmental lessons that have relevance to the questions involved in End of Days. But the lesson I like best illustrates the love of God and the intricate energies He gave that some call "systems" (and indeed they are), in a life story of a little bird.

XI

Lessons from A Super Bird

"When one tugs at a single thing in nature, he finds it attached to the rest of the world." (John Muir)

My backyard has become a great hatching area for sparrows. Each summer evening I watch flights of hundreds of them, flying across the yard to their roosting places in the Box Elders and Cedars. I call to them and wonder why they don't pay attention to me since I am the provider of approximately 25 pounds of seed for them every week. But they have resigned me to the role of observer and nothing more. Still, once in a while I spot a particular bird in the bush at my window who has fattened on my feed and preens a sleek brown feather coat. He is an athlete, only a couple of ounces in weight but a survivor in his bird world.

I am attracted to him because he reminds me of a world champion bird of incredible strength and brilliance who travels in a much more expansive realm, immeasurable by our means, up-and-down the entire planet Earth. By his conquering of it he is not only a victor but a messenger of the mystery and power of nature.

He is a mighty robin -sized shorebird, weighing in at 4 1/2 ounces, a Rufa red knot by classification. I discovered his story in a book

by Philip Hoose, Moon Bird: a Year on the Wind with the Great
Survivor B- 95.

Each February B-95 takes off with his flock of 1000+ Rufa red
knot companions from their winter ground in the Tierra del Fuego
(southern tip of South America) for a journey of 9000 miles to their
breeding ground in the Canadian Arctic. Late in summer they begin
the return journey, 9000 miles back to where they started.

Why do they do that? Why don't they stay in one place and live and
adapt as other creatures do? How are they able to navigate unerringly
such a journey? And a special question: B- 95 has made the journey
nearly 20 times; how much longer can he do it? What gives him such
amazing power and longevity?

There is more than one story involved with Moon Bird. There is the
individual survival story of B-95. There is the story of the great bird
migrations. There is the story of dedicated scientists such as Patricia
Gonzalez and Brian Harrington and their colleagues who bring the
glory of the red knots into our lives. And there is a looming story
of extinction.

In the 20 years B-95 has been flying, the Rufa red knot population
has declined by 80%. Bird scientists declare that the main reason for
the sharp decline is that the stopover sites for migratory shorebirds are
being littered with trash, dug up, polluted, poisoned and otherwise
degraded. It is a serious question if we shall see shorebirds in the
future.

Happening now is a mass distinction of many species. It is not the
first time in the history of the world that this has occurred. But
the extinction wave happening now is different: It may be likened
to the extermination of the American bison in the 19th century. At
the beginning of that century there were over 50 million Buffalo

roaming the planes. By the end of the century there were a few hundred left struggling for survival in the Yellowstone.

One species– Homo sapiens– is responsible for wiping out thousands of life forms by consuming more than half of the world's freshwater, radically altering the Earth's resources, and indiscriminate slaughter. Commandeers for new wells are no longer satisfied with the traditional methods of land and water exploitation. Now there are new techniques of hydraulic fracturing deep into the earth and the oceans without real knowledge or regard for long-term consequences. In this context, extinction of the shorebirds may be a minor consequence, hardly worth noticing.

Why should we care about shorebirds? Why care about anything that does not benefit us directly or give us pleasure? Before we were knowledgeable enough even to raise such questions, the American Indians knew the answer. Everything is connected! And behind the material things of this earth there is a Great Spirit that does not bless destruction or clumsy rearrangements of His creation.

Each species belongs to a complicated web of energy and activity called an eco- system. Together, these webs connect everything from the smallest, most obscure living things to the big trees and rivers and mountains, the kings of our environment. We do not know how these eco- systems can be unraveled or the consequences of that happening. Yet God gives us examples of the mystery and the power. One such example is the fascinating little Super Bird, B- 95.

Every life form is fascinating and mysterious in its own right, and each species with which we share the Earth is a success story. The Lord God made them all and made them to work according to His design. It's the responsibility of Homo sapiens to understand and protect them. And, yes, to enjoy them! just as I enjoy the sparrows in my backyard.

And just to replicate on the power of love, here is another story about another little bird, taken from "Sketches from the Underground", by Ivan Turgenov:

Only By Love

I was on my way home from hunting, and was walking up the garden Avenue. My dog was running in front of me. Suddenly he slackened his pace and began to steal forward as though he scented game ahead.

I looked along the Avenue, and I saw on the ground a young sparrow. It had fallen from the nest (a strong wind was blowing and shaking the birches of the avenue), and there it sat and never stirred, except to sketch out its little have grown wings in a helpless flutter.

My dog was slowly approaching it, when suddenly, darting from the tree overhead, an old black throated sparrow dropped like a stone right before his nose, and, all rumpled and flustered, with a plaintive desperate cry flung itself, once, twice, at his open jaws with their great teeth.

It would save its young one; it screened it with its own body; the tiny frame quivered with terror; the little cries grew wild and hoarse; it sank and died. It had sacrificed itself.

What a huge monster the dog must have seemed to it! And yet it could not stay up there on it's safe bough. A power stronger than its own will tore it away.

My dog stood still, and then slunk back disconcerted. Plainly, he too had to recognize that power. I called him to me, and a feeling of reverence came over me as I passed on.

Yes, do not laugh. It was really reverence I felt before that heroic little bird and the passionate outburst of its love.

Love, I thought, is verily stronger than death and the terror of death. By love, only by love, is life sustained and moved. (Ivan Turgenev)

****

There is a question about reality constantly before, so pervasive and so simple, it's on the lips of every child: "Do you love me?" Where does this come from?

XII

Cowardice and Courage

Are terrorists cowards? I don't usually agree with the comedian, Bill Maher, but I do grant that a comment he made on this topic is astute:" We have been the cowards, lobbing cruise missiles from 2000 miles away. That's cowardly. Staying in the airplane when it hits the building, say what you want about it, that's not cowardly. Stupid maybe but not cowardly."

If he had said, "Evil! but not cowardly, I could partially agree with him." The problem is, we could easily then get turned to the argument that the terrorists exhibit courage. That's bullshit!

I first wrote on this topic in 2004 in an article titled," Misbegotten Respect for Suicide Bombers." I reported on a worldwide conference of Islamic leaders whose major conclusion was that terrorism should be defined by the United Nations but then went on to proclaim that they were opposed to all forms of terrorism except the Palestinian suicide bombers: they were not terrorists, they were religious martyrs.

Here we have it all again: the deconstruction of logical thought combined with lack of any standard of humanity. How any religious leader can argue that intentional and indiscriminate killing not of soldiers but of innocent people, including children, is justifiable by a higher cause is indeed difficult to understand.

If the ongoing effort to define terrorism should exclude these heinous acts, it is hard to see anything but an apocalyptic end. Such a reigning religious doctrine– already being taught to eight-year-olds in Palestine– would bring the most brutish human condition the world has yet known. For if such a monstrous evil did dominate the human heart, how could there be any room for forgiveness and atonement?

Courage in the right classical sense is a virtue. What the terrorists do is not virtuous by any definition other than the hard left wing disposition to sophistry.

Until our moral discourse became so impoverished that we find it difficult to distinguish between good and evil, we could recognize the difference between the killing of innocents and defending them. Regardless of their claim of pursuing a noble religious cause, the terrorists are engaged in a great evil which is never justified nor neutralized by religious dogma!

I think that a terrorist may indeed be a tough bastard, and any soldier going up against him ought to take that into consideration, but he is never courageous and it is a perversion of our language, not to mention a slander of our first responders and the military to dignify his sin with that label.

There seems to be a tendency, at least in the European states who seek to justify their appeasement– and maybe cowardice– by allowing terrorists, and here in the U.S. traitors like Bowe Bergdahl, some lenience in their actions, which we all should know by now end up by slitting innocent people's throats and torturing children to death.

Why put up with this cognitive dissonance? Is it another aspect of our current ideological stupidity wrought by moral relativism and political correctness?

Let's not get caught in the soporific argument that a person may have desirable and undesirable traits at the same time. Maybe all honest people could admit to that, but I believe the honest man or woman would not confuse courage with an evil act if he/she knows the bloody facts.

XIII

Artificial Intelligence and the Singularity I

When I was a professor and dean of the college in the late 1960s, I joined the World Future Society and became an active member. By the late 1970s, I had grown disillusioned with the Society's agenda and dropped out. I thought then that preoccupation with artificial intelligence was a wrongfooted approach to invention of the future. I have since humbly changed my mind. But it was through that association that I first became aware of the significant differences between linear growth and exponential growth.

The lesson of exponential growth is well captured in a description of a lily pond which may grow plants at a seemingly innocent rate, doubling each day until half the pond is covered. The next doubling suddenly covers the entire pond. That is exponential growth. The effect has proven time and again in various activities, such as a bank savings account in which a 21-year-old puts aside $2000 a year, never touches it, and finds a yield of $1 million when he retires at age 65.

The significance of technological change that is now occurring exponentially is outlined by the brilliant computer scientist and forecaster, Raymond Kurzweil, in his "law of accelerating returns".

(For an immediate, penetrating description of Kurzweil's work, go to the web and click on The Singularity Is Near.)

While most people may be aware of sci-fi depictions of Artificial Intelligence (AI) creations in movies such as Matrix, Terminator, or I Robot (from Isaac Asimov), few are aware of the broader significance of AI in all phases of human endeavor. We are moving on rapidly from narrow AI to Artificial General Intelligence.

Ray Kurzweil and other AI scientists now see the coming of self-aware machines of super intelligence within the next 30 to 40 years, perhaps sooner. This will happen because of the event of Technological Singularity. Kurzweil defines the "Singularity" as a coming epoch, in which the pace of technological change will be so rapid, its impact so deep, that human life will be irreversibly transformed. "Although neither utopian nor dystopian, this epoch will transform the concepts that we rely on to give meaning to our lives, from our business models, to the cycle of human life, including death itself." (KURZWEIL)

Recently, Kurzweil was joined in his prediction of the Singularity by two prominent Artificial Intelligence experts, MIT Professor Patrick Winston, and Jurgen Schmidhuber, Chief Scientist of the company, NNAISENCE.

Schmidhuber states that he is confident that the Singularity "is just 30 years away, if the trend doesn't break, and there will be rather cheap computational devices that have as many connections in your brain, but are much faster. There is no doubt in my mind that AIs are going to become supersmart."

On the fiction side, Richard K. Morgan postulates in his book, "Altered Carbon," in the 25th century, "humankind has spread throughout the galaxy, monitored by the watchful eye of the UN.

While division in race, religion, and class still exist, advances in technology have redefined life itself. Now assuming one can afford the expensive procedure, a person's consciousness can be stored in a cortical stack at the base of the brain and easily downloaded into a new body (or "sleeve") making death nothing more than a minor blip on the screen." Remember, this is just science fiction, but interesting to contemplate?

Meanwhile, the phenomenon of accelerating returns continues. We are now beginning to reach the "knee of the exponential curve", which is the stage when the exponential trend quickly becomes explosive, and the curve shoots straight up.

Kurzweil believes that the Singularity will represent "the merger of our biological thinking and existence with our technology, resulting in a world that is still human but transcends our biological roots." He expects thinking machines to pass the "Turing test", meaning that nonbiological intelligence will be indistinguishable from our biological intelligence by 2029. The nonbiological intelligence will be thousands of times more powerful than our unaided intelligence. We shall depend vitally on these thinking machines.(Heavy stuff, isn't it? We shall see.)

What are the implications of such astounding development if it occurs? How shall we learn to live with these machines? Is there much to fear from them, as Asimov's story suggests? Or in considering the "nano bots" we now hear about regularly, are we in danger of destroying our world by allowing nanotechnology to proceed with the development of these microscopic, self replicating, mechanical structures? Will we lose control of the development of new creation? Is all of this fantastic discovery and invention playing God? What are the possibilities, and consequences, of a "neo Luddite" attempt to halt fantastic technological development? Are Kurzweil and other "singularitarians" wrong in the first place, as some critics argue? These are premier questions for everyone's future.

(Notes: An excellent movie on the mathematical genius, Alan Turing, was made in 2014. Ned Ludd led a worker uprising in late 19th century London to destroy all machines.)

XIV

Artificial Intelligence and the Singularity II

Throughout my career as an educator, I kept my graduate association with the U.S. Army Artillery School in Oklahoma. During my last visit there, I saw a tall, broad shouldered sergeant walking down the stair, with an artificial leg. I was stunned, and I believe you will see the significance. In conversation with them I learned that he was preparing to go back to Iraq as a functioning squad leader. The prosthetic device he is using is driven by microprocessors at each joint, just one of many new applications that permit amputees who previously would have been unable even to lead normal civilian lives now to return to the battlefield. In one sense the sergeant is a special soldier, yet in a broader context of how our army is developing, he is not extraordinary.

U.S. Army Research, in conjunction with DARPA, is working on a "super warrior," 10 of which would be equivalent to today's brigade. They will have an exoskeleton that allows them to carry 180 pounds as though it were 5 pounds, run and leap like track stars, and will be plugged into a Pentagon grid. Add this new hardware capacity to predator drones. Combine this with new "smart artillery" which is deadly accurate and very fast, yet even these recent developments pale in comparison with the robot army coming.

In this new era, the military robots will have the intelligence to make battlefield decisions that presently belong to humans. They will have significant cognitive advantages over human soldiers. Herein lies the danger that the US Office of Naval Research is now carefully considering. The perception that robots will only do what humans have programmed them to do falls apart in at least two ways: it fails to take account of artificial intelligence becoming Artificial General Intelligence, and second, that programs are no longer written and understood by a single person. There are teams of programmers, none of whom know the entire program, so no one can predict how large programs will interact without testing in the field, an action unavailable to designers of military robots.

This does not mean that the robots cannot learn a warrior code, just as our human soldiers have done through superb training. But it will be a dramatic undertaking and immensely important to develop the ethical dimension if we are to avoid the peril projected by Asimov in his story, I, Robot. Can this be done? Probably, but not certainly. Could we simply stop the development entirely? Perhaps, but not likely.

The dilemma posed here is but one of several to a future of continuing exponential growth– ironically, dilemmas which may depend on nonbiological super intelligence to resolve. The likelihood is that in full maturity, today's kids shall either learn to coexist with subservient robots and conscious machines or face a battle for survival against these super intelligent machines turned psychotic.

But God is with us! Face the existential fact that life is a challenge!

The AI fantasies imagined by science fiction writers have not materialized, at least not yet, but AI is already in more common usage than many people realize. As Nick Bostrom, another AI scientist, has pointed out, AI inspired systems are already integral to many everyday technologies, such as Internet search engines, bank software for processing transactions, software for large inventories, and in medical diagnosis.

My generation has exemplified adaptation to rapid technological change, even those of us who are not technically savvy.(I tell my grandson that I am basically a Luddite.)

Consider these developments of the past 30 years: the Personal Computer; communications greatly enhanced by fax machines in the late 1980s;and then by the Internet, invented by US government, but exploited tremendously by entrepreneurs in the private sector. At the same time on the bionic front, I know a man with two artificial knees and two artificial hips;the quality of his life is far beyond what it would have been 50 years ago.

As computers became more powerful, they also became correspondingly less expensive to all, and smaller in the bargain. In the near future they will look like pens that we carry in our pockets. Now it is almost standard that everyone has access to a computer. Of course, there are issues, loss of privacy, for example, but we have learned to adapt and adjust in relatively easy fashion. Our world changed and we changed with it. But there is a dialectic at work here too. We ordinary people did not see much of this coming. We are like passengers facing backwards on a train hurtling with even greater speed into the future.

What my generation has experienced is mild on the growth curve compared with what the next generation shall face. The issues will become much more profound, going to the very heart of what it means to be human. The first question is, can a machine of nonbiological intelligence become self-conscious?

Kurzweil, Bostrum, and other singulartarians are convinced that such an event will happen within the next half-century.

If so, how can humans ensure that these super intelligent machines are benevolent allies of humankind? What strategies and policies need to be considered now in order to ensure that the relationships between humans and machines will be positive? What are the prospects for, and the potential consequences, of trans-humanism—the merging of machines and humans in the same entity?

Where is God in the equation for whatever shall evolve?

If we view the dangers as too great to allow continuing technological development, what are our options? Can we stop these trends? I think perhaps we may indeed modify our directions of development in the sense that we have always played a role in our evolution, but that the evidence is too overwhelming contrarily to think that we can, or should, place extreme barriers in the path of science and technology as it seeks to discover how Intelligence is flooding our world.

So far in human history, science and technology have steadily advanced, sometimes with quantum leaps. Science has a natural overarching capability to go around irrational obstacles. The long-term trend of technological innovation is perpetual advancement.

As Ray Kurzweil says, "Only technology can provide the scale to overcome the challenges with which society struggled for generations. Emerging technologies will provide the means of providing and storing clean and renewable energy, removing toxins and pathogens from our bodies and the environment, and providing the knowledge and wealth to overcome hunger and poverty."

It is an awesome challenge. If there are moments when the load becomes too much to bear, "Choose something like a star... to stay the mind upon."(Robert Frost)

XV

Artificial Intelligence and the Singularity III

When the Singularity comes, as I believe it will, another great leap in the evolutionary process will change our world in a manner similar to the human species becoming self-aware eons ago. When that was exactly we cannot know, but it was then that God created us in His image, not physically but spiritually, with a capacity for moral choice and creative design.

Whether or not our new self-aware creations, thinking machines, will have a soul is a subject of debate in the community of artificial intelligence scientists. The level of intelligence they will bring is also debatable, but most projections place it much higher than our own. There is an important difference tween our evolution and there's: we did not create ourselves, but we are the agents creating these machines, at least until such time as they supersede us in their replication. In this sense we are a partner in the evolutionary process.

With the emergence of the human soul, there is a different kind of deity which begins to express itself, not to spare humankind from the "problem of evil," but to provide guidance, compassion, and the healing power of love. In our conscience and experience we can find the highest, noblest expression of this love. In the words of St. John,

"The word was made flesh, and dwelt among us, and we beheld his glory, the glory of the only begotten of the Father, full of grace and truth."

I agree with those who contend that this belief can only be taken on faith. There is a distinction between God as Creator and God as Love. The mystery of the difference between physical evolution and spiritual evolution is magnified by its receding dialectical nature and the upending unity of all forces, "the all in all of Christ."

On what basis can we believe these things? Is it science, or religion, or philosophy? I contend for, and urge readers to think seriously about, a new ground being formed which authentically combines science and faith in the invention of the brave new world through artificial intelligence. Faith in a loving God left out of the equation for guidance and wisdom is an omission potentially devastating.

Expand the term to Artificial General Intelligence. Artificial intelligence has been with us for more than four decades in ways we now take for granted. But when you have an AI system that can assist in the design of improved versions of itself, you could go overnight to something radically super intelligent.(See Bostrom)

Unity is our watchword in dealing with Artificial General Intelligence, unity of human beings and super intelligent machines. I am not thinking of trans-humanism here, although some AI experts like Kurzweil envision that kind of development, but obviously our challenge as creators will be to help ensure that ultimate loyalty is structured into the "soul" of these machines, not simply as an Asimov rule, but as part of a mutually held moral and ethical consciousness given to us by God.

Can a machine understand its human organs, its history? Even more charismatic, can a machine become aware of God's presence? It remains to be seen, but there are reasons to believe that, aided by super intelligence, humankind may reach a higher ground spiritually and materially than we have ever known before. The opposite would surely be the end of days.

End Notes

What are your personal beliefs? I believe in the Holy Trinity. I believe in the institutions of marriage and family. I believe in the U.S. Constitution and the Bill of Rights. I believe in protecting women and children and the environment. I believe that truth ultimately wins out over lies.

Is there anything else you believe? If you want to play around, here's a list possibly to consider:

I believe there's no business like show business, and nothing like a Dame, prosperity is just around the corner, the only thing we have to fear is fear itself, this generation has a rendezvous with destiny, when more and more people are thrown out of work unemployment results, necessity is the mother of invention, the Iceman cometh, the postman always rings twice, and Kilroy was here.

Face the music: Illecitimus non carborundum!

I believe in miracles, and that only God can make a tree, and there will be bluebirds over the white cliffs of Dover tomorrow when the world is free, and that anyone who goes to a psychiatrist ought to have his head examined.

I would rather be right then be president, and I would rather see a purple cow then be one.

Don't shoot the messenger, and don't give up the ship, and don't tread on me.

Go and do the right thing, with love.

****

Rich Lowry's article, "Considering Our Fracking Future," 7/10/13, reveals with rich irony the Orwellian methods of "journalists," like Lowry, to dissuade us from finding the truth. Orwellian interpretations of what's going on abound, and are astonishingly successful in disarming people. It could be said more simply that these are lies, but that misses the process of how it's done. Press and government agents do not tell lies; after all, they have a responsibility to clarify events and provide more nuanced explanations. Some shape of the truth still exists. Thus, we are suborned and more careful about drawing critical conclusions because we want to believe in our government and in a free and responsible press.

Here's a key question: what should be the highest priority of our government– citizen rights to protection? or business proprietary rights? The question was answered in 2005 when the Safe Drinking Water Act was amended to exempt fracking.

The American leaders I admire most are Abraham Lincoln, George Washington, Robert E. Lee, John Muir, Martin Luther King Jr, and the great Lakota Chief, Tashunko Witco (Crazy Horse). But I also admire Great Britain's Prime Minister, Winston Churchill, whom I consider to be the greatest man of the 20ᵗʰ century.

The greatest of the English speaking poets were Robert Burns, a Scotsman, William Butler Yeats, an Irishman, Dylan Thomas, a Welshman, Emily Dickinson and Robert Frost, American, Rainer

Maria Rilke, a German, and Alfred Lord Tennyson, an Englishman (oh well, one is better than none.)

Ben Johnson and the man from Stratford:" No, Ben, it's all nothing. We come, we go, and when were done we're done... When he talks like that, there's nothing for a man to do, but lead him somewhere for a drink."

Yeats said it, "the worst thing about some men is that when they are not drunk they are sober." Reminds me of Churchill at a party when he was drunk and argued with a lady. Churchill lost his cool and said "Madam, you are just ugly." She immediately replied, "you, sir, are drunk!" He replied just as quick, "yes, you're right about that, but I will be sober in the morning."

My favorite athletes were Stan Musial, Ted Williams, Johnny Unitas, Joe Montana, Bobby Orr, Gil Perrault, Steve Nash, Cal Ripken, Mariano Rivera, Derek Jeter, Peyton Manning. I liked the St. Louis Cardinals when I was young, and the New York Yankees when I was old.

A wild bird, tossed into flight of no beginning and uncertain end, some time belief suspended but ultimately steady in faith and flight, admits his errors and sins on this earth before a loving God; as for those who were loved, or were wronged, he cannot tell you now; when the winds drive and whirl and blow him along no longer, maybe then, some better time.

I look for the heavenly Elysian fields, the solitude and elegance of reconciliation.

JOH: 3/1/18 Cursom Perficio

St. Patrick

Revered as the patron saint of the Irish, Patrick was not Irish. His birthplace and year of birth are not actually known. He was born somewhere in Great Britain, either Scotland or Wales.

At the age of 15, he was kidnapped by some Irish Pirates, and sold into slavery in Ireland. He served as a slave for six years, handling sheep herds for his master.

His life as a shepherd, was endless misery. Left alone with the sheep in the hills, he was cold, hungry to the point of starvation.

But this was also a time, when his soul surged: He went deep into his inner self to gain spiritual command. He realized there was more to this beautiful land with its lush green hills.

Did he drive out the snakes in Ireland? The factual answer is no. There were never any snakes in Ireland, but there is also a spiritual answer. While on his green hillside with his sheep, he began to think that he was not a good person. He reached out and found his Lord, Jesus Christ.

Then by God's grace, he was able to escape and return to his earlier home. He had fallen in love with Ireland, and after a visit to Rome, returned to his adopted country as a missionary. He is celebrated and honored on March 17 for bringing the light of Jesus Christ to the people of Ireland.

Acknowledgements

I remain indebted to sources and citations listed in my previous iUniverse books, Reading Yeats and Striving to Be a College President, and Chasing Crazy Horse I and II.

I also acknowledge the following for this work:

John O. Hunter, For the Love of Poetry, Amazon Create Space, 2009

Robert Louis Wilken, "Christianity Face to Face with Islam", First Things, 2010

Dean Miller, Deep State, American Survivor, 2017

Yuval Noah Harari, sapiens, A History of Humankind, Amazon Audible Book

Yuval Noah Harari, Homo Deus, Amazon Audible Book

George Orwell, 1984, New Classical Edition, Amazon Audible Book

Pierre Teilhard de Chardin, The Divine Milieu, Amazon Kindle Edition

Jordan B. Peterson, 12 Rules for Life: Antidote for Chaos, YouTube

Lettters and Articles from Judicial Watch

Ancient Christian Wisdom, files, Word Press.com, 2014

I am also pleased to acknowledge technical assistance in the manuscript development from my grandson, Angelo Maldonado

JOH

Printed in the United States
by Baker & Taylor Publisher Services